This is a drum kit.

a drummer

1

Drums can be struck with the hands...

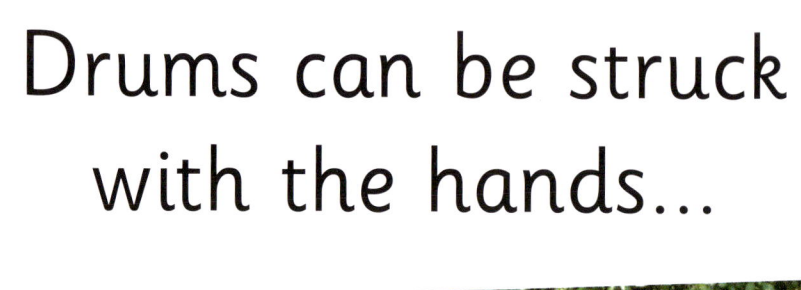

...or with drumsticks.

Drumsticks can be hard and wooden...

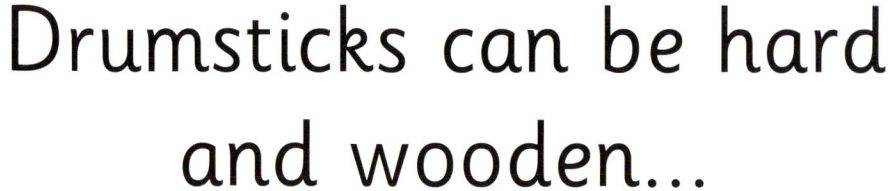

...soft, with felt at the end...

felt

brush

...or brushes.

Different sorts of drums:

conga

African drums

Drums can be electric, too.

an electric drum kit